C000199951

Weeds
by Roger Phillips

assisted by Martyn Rix
and Jacqui Hurst

Elm Tree Books London

INTRODUCTION

Aim

In this book we have aimed to photograph and describe 100 of the commonest or more beautiful weeds found in the British Isles and northern Europe.

How to use this book

The weeds are arranged roughly in their order of flowering, and the actual date of the photograph is given on the caption. In most cases one photograph shows the most important parts of the plant, laid out so that details of flowers and leaves can be seen easily and clearly. The other shows either a seedling, in the case of commoner weeds, so they may be recognised and removed before they flower or, in the case of rarer cornfield weeds, the growing plant. Sometimes, two closely related or similar species are shown together, and the distinctions between them are mentioned in the text.

What is a weed?

A weed has been neatly defined as a plant growing where it is not wanted. Some of the most obnoxious weeds such as Winter Heliotrope or Ground Elder were introduced into gardens as ornamental or medicinal plants. Other weeds such as Cornflower and Larkspur were formerly common in cornfields, but are now very rare and are grown in gardens as ornamental annuals.

The Photographs

The studio photographs were taken on a Bronica 120 format with a 75mm lens. Scale: ○ is 1cm. The field photographs were taken on a Nikon FM camera with a 50mm lens, occasionally with close-up attachments. The film was Kodak Ektachrome 64 ASA in both cases, but when used outdoors it was pushed one stop in development.

Mixed poppies in an abandoned strawberry field (see p. 113)

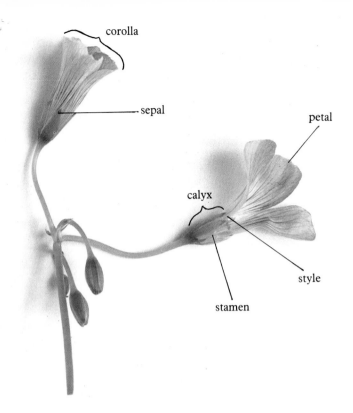

corolla

sepal

petal

calyx

style

stamen

Glossary

apomictic   a plant in which seeds are formed without normal fertilisation taking place: the progeny are all genetically identical to the mother plant

awns   stiff, bristle-like hairs which project from the spikelets of a grass

bifid   divided into two

cleistogamous   specialised, usually very small flowers which set seed without opening

lanceolate   shaped like a lance, wider towards the base

inflorescence   the part of the plant which bears the flowers

panicle   a branched inflorescence, often of a grass

pinnate   with leaflets on either side of a central stem

stolon   underground shoot producing new plant

tuber   underground swollen rootstock

Winter Heliotrope photographed 9 January

Winter Heliotrope photographed 6 May

Winter Heliotrope

Petasites fragrans (daisy family) was introduced from the western Mediterranean in 1808, and is now found almost throughout Britain, usually in old gardens, but also by roadsides where it forms large patches, smothering all other vegetation. It was treasured by Victorian gardeners, and is still by the unwary even today, as a mid-winter flower with a sweet heavy scent. Most of them, however, must have rued the day they bought it, and their successors have not ceased to curse them. The round leaves can be up to 20cm across. Hardy underground stems can spread as much as 3 feet in a year, and each broken piece can regrow into a new plant. It is worst in heavy soil and although the tops may be killed by hard winters it soon grows again from below ground. Even modern weedkillers such as Glycosate 'Roundup' or 'Tumbleweed' need to be applied several times before every piece is killed.

Hairy Bittercress photographed 5 April

Hairy Bittercress seedling photographed 10 February

Hairy Bittercress

Cardamine hirsuta (cabbage family) is one of the commonest annual garden weeds and one of the earliest to flower, usually opening in March and in seed by April. Because it flowers and ripens seed so quickly, the gardener can easily miss it, and often pulls at its seed head, only to trigger off the explosive seed pods and scatter the seed. It is often called 'Jumping Cress', and its seeds have been shown to be ejected as far as 80cm from the parent plant; a good specimen can produce 50,000 seeds. The seeds usually germinate in autumn, and the rosette of compound leaves remains green through the hardest winters. Other generations are produced through the summer in wet weather. Hairy Bittercress is found throughout the British Isles, and across the northern hemisphere, both as a weed and as a wild plant in dry rocky places, and screes in the mountains.

7

Coltsfoot photographed 16 March

Coltsfoot photographed 10 June

Coltsfoot

Tussilago farfara (daisy family) is a common weed by roadsides, especially on new embankments, and in gardens. Its beautiful yellow flowers appear in March or early April, grouped in dense, leafless tufts emerging out of bare soil. The flower heads can be picked and used to make wine. The large leaves emerge a few weeks later; formerly they were dried, and smoked as a remedy for coughs. As a persistent garden weed Coltsfoot is as bad as Winter Heliotrope, its fleshy roots penetrating the subsoil and resisting all but the deepest digging. It can also spread by seed. Weedkillers such as Glycosate should be sprayed or painted on to the leaves, and several applications may be needed.

Coltsfoot is found throughout the British Isles, across Asia, and south to North Africa, especially in the mountains where it is characteristic of soil recently laid bare by rockfalls or landslides.

Chickweed photographed 19 March

Chickweed seedling photographed 10 February

Chickweed

Stellaria media (carnation family) is a very common annual weed in gardens, by roadsides or on any bare ground. It can vary in size from a tiny single-stemmed plant with a few leaves and flowers, to a lush, prostrate, wide-spreading and rooting plant covering about 1 square metre. Chickweed makes good bird-food, and can also be eaten raw in salads, as all parts of the plant are edible.

Flowers can be found on Chickweed at all times of the year, and it is not noticably more frequent in early spring than in summer or autumn. It is found commonly throughout the British Isles, indeed throughout the world in temperate areas.

One closely-related species, *S. pallida* (*S. apetala*), **Lesser Chickweed**, is found throughout Europe, especially on sandy soils. It has either minute petals or none at all, and the sepals are smaller, 2–3.5mm, against 4.5–5mm in *S. media*, and it has 1–3, not 3–7 stamens.

Left to right *Caucasian Speedwell; Buxbaum's Speedwell; Grey Speedwell; Ivy Speedwell*, photographed 10 June

Caucasian Speedwell photographed 4 May

Speedwells

Veronica species (figwort family) can be recognised by their usually blue flowers, which have 2 stamens and 4 lobes, the upper large, rounded and usually veined, the lower smaller.

Ivy Speedwell (*V. hederifolia*), is a common annual plant with long trailing hairy stems and small, pale purplish, long-stalked flowers. **Buxbaum's Speedwell** (*V. persica*) was not known here until 1825. A common annual, it has yellowish-green leaves and largish, bright blue flowers 8–12mm across, with a paler lower lobe. **Caucasian Speedwell** (*V. filiformis*) was introduced from the Caucasus as a rock garden plant though here it has found mown lawns to be its perfect habitat and owes some of its success to its being resistant to the weedkiller 2–4D. **Grey Speedwell** (*V. polita*) is like a small flowered *V. persica*. An annual, it has greyish leaves and medium-sized bright blue flowers 4–8mm across, all the petals equally coloured.

Shepherd's Purse photographed 5 April

Shepherd's Purse photographed 5 April

Shepherd's Purse

Capsella bursa-pastoris (cabbage family) is a very common annual weed throughout the world in gardens, fields and by roadsides, on all types of soil. It is easily recognised by its purse-shaped seed pods which consist of two pouches separated by a narrowly oval membrane, which is all that remains once the seeds have fallen.

Shepherd's Purse can be found in flower at any time of year, but most commonly in spring, from rosettes which have survived the winter. The basal leaves are very variable in shape, from deeply dissected to entire, and the seed pods also vary in shape and in the number of seeds they contain.

Dandelion photographed 10 April

Dandelion photographed 20 April

Dandelion

Taraxacum officinale (daisy family) is one of the most conspicuous and familiar of garden weeds and is also common along roads, and in wet or dry meadows. Its deep taproot always breaks when pulled up and even the thin piece left behind soon grows into a new plant. It can however be killed by spraying with hormone weedkillers such as 2–4D.

Dandelions are found throughout the British Isles and around the northern hemisphere. In different habitats they vary greatly, in size, leaf shape, bracts and flower heads. Most are apomictic (that is they set seed without normal fertilisation so that all seedlings are like the mother plant) thus any small differences persist, and hundreds of microspecies have been described. Young Dandelion leaves make an excellent slightly bitter salad and are very popular in France and Belgium where they are called *Pissenlit*, wet-a-bed.

Groundsel photographed 10 April

Groundsel seedling photographed 8 July

Groundsel

Senecio vulgaris (daisy family) is one of the commonest garden weeds, especially on damper heavy soils. It is an annual and can flower and fruit at any time of year. Most of the seeds shed can germinate within a week, and the seedlings can themselves be producing seed in five weeks. Thus one seed can theoretically produce a thousand million plants between spring and autumn.

The fruits are very light and can be carried long distances on their pappus parachutes; they also become sticky when wet and can stick to the feet of animals or birds. Goldfinches, sparrows and other seed-eating birds are especially fond of the seeds and some pass through and still germinate. Dispersal is thus very efficient and Groundsel is now found throughout the temperate parts of the world.

Annual Meadow Grass photographed 19 March

Annual Meadow Grass photographed 12 July

Annual Meadow Grass

Poa annua (grass family) is the commonest of the annual grasses, and is found in all sorts of bare ground. Like most annuals it varies greatly in size according to the amount of water it receives and the fertility of the soil, but it is usually small, under 15cm high and characteristically bright yellowish-green, though sometimes with purplish spikelets. Seeds germinate and the plants flower at any time of year, though most commonly in spring.

Annual Meadow Grass grows throughout the British Isles, and Europe, especially in the south. It can be recognised as a *Poa* by its spikelets which do not have awns, and is distinguished from other *Poa* species by being dwarf and annual without creeping underground shoots, and by its branching panicles and soft texture.

Evergreen Alkanet photographed 20 April

Evergreen Alkanet seedling photographed 16 March

Evergreen Alkanet

Pentaglottis sempervirens (borage family) is another old-fashioned garden plant, now usually found as a weed, and, what is worse, a weed that seeds itself freely on any type of soil and is very hard to eradicate because of its deep brittle root which quickly regenerates if broken. The seedlings appear in late spring; the rich blue flowers usually in April and May, though if the plant is cut down after flowering, a second crop of flowers will appear. The leaves and stems are bristly hairy, and reach a height of about 50cm.

Alkanet is a native of southern Europe, from south-west Portugal and Spain to south-west France, but is widely naturalised in the British Isles, especially in the south-west and near the sea, as well as in Belgium and Italy.

Spotted Medick photographed 19 May

Black Medick; young plants photographed 8 May

Medicks

Medicago arabica, **Spotted Medick**, and *M. lupulina*, **Black Medick**, are small yellow-flowered clover-like members of the pea family. They may be distinguished from true clovers such as Shamrock or Lesser Trefoil (*Trifolium dubium*) by their seed pods which are often coiled and usually longer than the calyx. Spotted Medick has a reddish spot in the middle of each leaflet and flowers in a loose head; its seed pod is coiled and curved with hooked spines.

Black Medick has unmarked leaflets and flowers in a dense head; its seed pods are small, black and one-seeded. Other medicks are rare weeds, usually found on sandy soils, especially near the sea.

Both Spotted Medick and Black Medick are annuals. The seeds germinate in spring. Both are common in the south of England, but Spotted Medick is rare in the north, in Ireland, and in northern Europe.

Bugloss photographed 1 June

Bugloss showing winter rosette photographed 19 May

Bugloss

Anchusa arvensis (borage family) is an annual with bristly, hairy leaves and small, pale blue forget-me-not-like flowers, with white scales in the throat. The plant is usually bushy, spreading and between 15–40cm high, flowering from May onwards. The leaves have hairs with a conspicuous pale swollen base, and an undulating margin. When not flowering Bugloss might be confused with **Viper's Bugloss** which has rosettes of rather similar but narrower bristly-haired leaves; Viper's Bugloss (*Echium vulgare*) is a biennial, a robuster plant and produces an upright inflorescence of rich blue tubular flowers, pink in bud, with protruding stamens. Bugloss is found throughout the British Isles and Europe, most commonly on sandy soils, usually growing in arable fields, but is becoming rare because of the efficiency of selective agricultural weedkillers.

Red Dead-nettle photographed 20 April

Red Dead-nettle; young plant photographed 19 March

Red Dead-nettle

Lamium purpureum (dead-nettle family) is a very common annual throughout Europe and the British Isles. Its flowers open in early spring and it can then remain in flower for the rest of the summer. The flowering stems are at most about 25cm high, and the flowers open in succession, in the axils of the upper leaves.

Three other related dead-nettles are rather rare; **Henbit**, *Lamium amplexicaule*, is commoner on light soils, its leaves are more rounded and it has both small cleistogamous flowers and large normal ones which differ from those of Red Dead-nettle by having no hairs inside the base of the corolla tube. A third species, *L. molucellifolium*, is commoner in Scotland. It has a long calyx (8–12mm), with teeth longer than the tube. The fourth, *L. hybridum* differs from *L. purpureum* in its deeply dentate leaves and bracts.

White Dead-nettle photographed 15 June

White Dead-nettle; overwintering plants photographed 10 July

White Dead-nettle

Lamium album (dead-nettle family) is a perennial which, if neglected, will form loose patches by means of its spreading, rooting stolons. Its white flowers appear in late spring and are much sought after by bumble-bees whose long tongues can reach the nectar. They also help distinguish it from the Stinging Nettle which has minute inconspicuous flowers, and it has even been suggested that White Dead-nettle owes some of its success as a weed to its similarity to the Stinging Nettle; ignorant people are afraid to pull it up! The seeds have an oily lump on them which is attractive to ants and probably aids their dispersal.

White Dead-nettle is found throughout the British Isles, but it is rare or absent in the north of Scotland and in Ireland except in the north-east. On the Continent it is common, but rarer in the south.

Fumitory photographed 20 April

Fumitory

Fumaria officinalis (fumitory family) is a scrambling annual found in arable
fields, gardens and any disturbed ground throughout the British Isles, but
is commoner in the east. On the Continent, it is recorded everywhere
except on some of the islands. The whole plant is soft and fleshy; the leaves
are glaucous green, the flowers various shades and combinations of
purplish-pink or white. The seeds germinate in spring, and in moist fertile
soil can soon make a large spreading plant. Flowering is from May
onwards.

Several other species are rather rarer. *F. occidentalis* is confined to
Cornwall. It has large, whitish and purple flowers. *F. bastardii* and
F. capreolata are also large flowered and commoner in the far west of
England and throughout Ireland. Other small-flowered species *F. densi-
flora*, *F. vaillentii* and *F. parviflora* are confined to the chalk in south-east
England.

33

Teesdalia photographed 15 April

Whitlow Grass photographed 12 March

Whitlow Grass, Teesdalia

Erophila verna (cabbage family) is an annual which produces a tiny rosette of leaves in autumn and flowers in early spring, usually in March and April. It can be recognised by its deeply divided white petals and its ovate or rounded seed pods on long slender stems. The whole plant is rarely more than 5cm high when flowering, taller when in fruit.

Teesdalia nudicaulis (cabbage family) is similar in general appearance but has pinnate leaves with rounded lobes, petals undivided with a blunt apex and heart-shaped seed pods attached at the point.

Neither Whitlow Grass nor *Teesdalia* are very common, but are usually found on light sandy soils, especially near the sea, and are sometimes common in natural open habitats such as stable sand dunes. They are found throughout the British Isles and on the Continent everywhere except in the Arctic.

Greater Celandine photographed 18 May

Greater Celandine photographed 18 May

Greater Celandine

Chelidonium majus (poppy family) is a common weed in old gardens as it was formerly grown for its medicinal properties. Its orange-yellow juice, which contains alkaloids, was used as a remedy for warts, and an infusion of its leaves as a purgative. It is not related to the Common Celandine – the only similarity is in the small bright yellow flowers.

Greater Celandine is a perennial, but individual plants are not long lived, and it seeds itself freely in flower beds, paths, and along hedges. It flowers from May to August. The seeds are black and shiny, with a white appendage which is attractive to ants.

Greater Celandine is not native to the British Isles, but is commonly naturalised; it is probably native in southern Europe and Asia, but is now found from Sweden southwards, and is known to have been present in Sussex before the last ice age.

Sticky Mouse-ear Chickweed photographed 20 April

Sticky Mouse-ear Chickweed seedling photographed 23 April

Sticky or Clustered Mouse-ear Chickweed

Cerastium glomeratum (carnation family) is a very common plant in open places such as gardens, arable fields, by roadsides, on old walls and waste ground, and on sand dunes. It is an annual, germinating in autumn and flowering in spring. The plant is covered with soft hairs, some of which are sticky with glands so that it often becomes coated with particles of earth or sand. The flowers are always in a tight head, hence the name '*glomeratum*', and the flower stalks do not elongate in fruit. The flowers are probably self-pollinating, but may even be cleistogamous. Other annual mouse-ear chickweeds, *C. semidecandrum* and *C. atrovirens*, are smaller plants with solitary flowers and capsules on long stalks, which in *C. semidecandrum* are bent downwards. They are commonest in dry sandy places, especially on dunes, by the sea.

Thale Cress photographed 23 April

Thale Cress; winter rosette photographed 20 February

Thale Cress

Arabidopsis thaliana (cabbage family) is a very common annual weed on all types of soil. It is found throughout the British Isles, on dry and heavy soils, in gardens, arable fields and waste places. On the Continent also it is a universal weed, and it has spread throughout the world. The seed usually germinates in autumn and the plant over-winters as a rosette of rather purplish, sparsely hairy leaves. The flower stem is upright and the flowers open from March onwards. It can be distinguished from other small similar white-flowered annuals by its seed pods which are narrow and almost straight, held out at an angle from the stem on spreading stalks.

Thale Cress has been known to complete its life cycle from germination to seeding in as little as four weeks and most strains have been found to require short days for flowering.

Parsley Piert photographed 8 May

Parsley Piert seedling photographed 24 October

Parsley Piert

Aphanes arvensis (rose family) is a dwarf creeping plant, with deeply cut leaves and insignificant green flowers. It is commonest on acid sandy soils in the spring as most seeds germinate with the autumn rains, and the plant grows through the winter before flowering.

Two species are common in the British Isles; *A. arvensis*, which is frequently found on both sandy acid and chalky soils, and *A. microcarpa*, which grows only on acid soils. *A. microcarpa* is usually greener and more slender, with smaller fruit, 1.4–1.8mm as opposed to 2.2–2.6mm in *A. arvensis*, and calyx lobes which converge not spread.

Both species are common on the Continent, and *A. microcarpa* is found throughout the world. They are closely related to the Lady's Mantles, and are sometimes included in the genus *Alchemilla*. The name Parsley Piert refers to the parsley-like appearance of the plant, but is also a corruption of the French *Percepierre*.

Heartsease photographed 12 June

Heartsease seedling photographed 5 April

Heartsease or Wild Pansy

Viola arvensis and *Viola tricolor* are the wild pansies found in arable fields, grassy waste places, and as garden weeds throughout the British Isles, flowering in spring and summer.

V. arvensis, the **Field Pansy**, is an annual which usually has small pale creamy-yellow flowers less than 10mm across, but sometimes has larger flowers with blue on some of the petals. It is common throughout the British Isles.

V. tricolor, the **Wild Pansy**, has much larger flowers, about 15mm across, with some or all the petals blue or purple. It is usually a perennial, if conditions are suitable, often forming patches about 30cm across, and may be very beautiful. It is much rarer in the south of England than *V. arvensis*, but is common in Scotland, usually in grassy places or in crops of rye grass. On the Continent it is also widespread, as far east as the Himalavas.

Hairy Vetch photographed 15 May

Common Vetch photographed 15 May

Vetches

Vicia hirsuta, **Hairy Vetch** or **Tare**, is easily recognised by its very small pale blue flowers (3–5mm long) 6–8 in a loose head, and 2-seeded hairy pods. The closely related *V. tetrasperma*, **Smooth Tare**, (shown left) has fewer, slightly larger flowers (5–7mm long), and 3 or 4 seeds in a smooth pod. Both flower from May to August and are found commonly in England, but *V. tetrasperma* is rare in northern Scotland and in Ireland. Neither are now serious weeds, but in the past they were some of the worst weeds, as they completely smothered the corn. Smooth Tare seeds have been found in deposits of grain from the Middle Ages, and as far back as Roman times and the late Bronze Age.

   Vicia sativa, **Common Vetch**, (above) is also very common in grassy places throughout the British Isles, and as a cornfield weed.

Corn Salad photographed 3 May

Corn Salad seedling photographed 2 April

Corn Salad or Lamb's Lettuce

Valerianella locusta (valerian family) is found throughout the British Isles and Europe in dry fields, on old walls and rocks and in gardens. It is an annual, germinating in autumn and remaining through the winter as a rosette of rounded pale green leaves. The minute, bright but pale blue flowers are in a tight flat-topped head. The seeds are rounded, flattened and corky on one side. Other species of Corn Salad are rarer, and may be most easily distinguished by their fruits which are narrower and less flattened.

As its name suggests, Lamb's Lettuce is edible, and can be eaten as an early spring salad; it has little flavour and a rather slimy texture. On the Continent however, a different species *V. olitoria* is commonly grown as a winter salad. This has a better flavour and in Switzerland, where it is popular, is called *Nüsslisalad*, nutty salad. In France it is called *Salade de Prêtre*, and is associated with Lent.

49

Charlock photographed 15 May

Charlock photographed 15 June

Charlock, Wild Mustard
Sinapis arvensis (cabbage family) is the commonest of the wild yellow
mustards which are found as weeds in waste places and arable fields. It is
common throughout the British Isles, and all over Europe eastwards to
Siberia. It has also spread, as a weed, to all other temperate parts of the
world. It can be distinguished from other yellow-flowered, mustard-like
plants as it is roughly hairy all over, with lanceolate and toothed upper
leaves, and fruits which have 3–7 veins and a long, conical, not flattened
beak. The many-veined fruit and somewhat larger petals distinguish
Charlock from the rather similar Black Mustard (*Brassica nigra*). The
somewhat rarer White Mustard (*Sinapis alba*), can be recognised by the
flattened beak of its fruit. Like so many cornfield weeds, Charlock is now
much less of a pest to farmers than before the days of selective weedkillers
when it could colour fields yellow in May.

Annual Pearlwort photographed 11 June

Procumbent Pearlwort photographed 10 July

Pearlwort

Sagina species (carnation family) can be recognised by their needle-like, short green leaves with a sharp point, and minute flowers with 4 green sepals and 4 minute white petals, opening from May onwards.

The annual *S. apetala*, which means 'without petals', is slender and more or less upright with minute petals and blunt sepals, and a capsule which remains upright until it is ripe. It is common on old walls, and as a garden weed on dry light soils throughout the British Isles except for the far north. The perennial, *S. procumbens*, has creeping rooting shoots, and short ascending flowering ones. The central rosette never flowers; the sepals are very rounded and the stalk of the young capsule is bent downwards. It is common on damp soils as a garden weed, or in lawns and is found in damp grassland throughout the British Isles and all round the northern hemisphere.

Left *Common Forget-me-not;* right *Changing Forget-met-not photographed 10 June*

Common Forget-me-not seedling photographed 2 April

Forget-me-nots

Myosotis arvensis (borage family), **Field** or **Common Forget-me-not**, is a common garden or arable weed that is also found in woods and on open soil on dunes throughout the British Isles and Europe, and eastwards to Siberia and western Asia. It flowers in April and onwards through the summer. It is similar in general habit to the Garden or Wood Forget-me-not (*M. sylvatica*), but has more softly hairy leaves and smaller flowers up to 5mm in diameter. The corolla tube is also shorter than the calyx.

Myosotis discolor is sometimes known as **Changing Forget-me-not** as the minute flowers open yellow or white and become blue before dropping. It is commoner on light soils throughout the British Isles, sometimes as a garden or arable weed, but often on dunes or other sandy places. Its calyx lobes are covered with hooked hairs, and do not open so the whole flower with the nutlets trapped inside can act as a burr.

Pineapple Weed photographed 18 June

Pineapple Weed seedlings photographed 10 June

Pineapple Weed or Rayless Mayweed

Chamomilla suaveolens (daisy family) is better known to most botanists under the name *Matricaria matricarioides*. It is easily recognised by its typical mayweed-like leaves, and by its lack of 'petals' or ray florets. The sweet, somewhat pineapple-like smell is also easy to remember. It is found everywhere in the British Isles, along roads and muddy tracks, in gardens and especially in poorly drained places. It arrived in Britain probably from north-east Asia via Oregon and was first recorded in 1871, but to begin with spread only slowly. It was between 1900 and 1925 that it spread really fast, probably in mud caught in the treads of car tyres, before tarred roads had become universal.

It is now found in all temperate parts of the world, throughout Europe and in South America and New Zealand.

Corn Gromwell photographed 16 May

Corn Gromwell and Corn Buttercup (lower right) *photographed 16 May*

Corn Gromwell

Lithospermum arvense (borage family) is a rather rare weed of cornfields, especially on chalky soils in the south and east of England. It is even rarer and merely transient in the north and in Ireland. The name *Lithospermum* is derived from the Greek, meaning stone seed, and refers to the very hard seeds, which in this species are greyish and warty. *Lithospermum officinale* is rather similar, but is perennial and has white shiny seeds. It is also commonest on the chalk, but in grassy bushy places and hedges.

Shown also in the field picture are the small yellow flowers and spiny fruit of **Corn Buttercup** (*Ranunculus arvensis*). This was formerly common in chalky cornfields in southern England, but has recently become very rare.

White Campion photographed 16 May

White Campion photographed 16 May

White Campion

Silene alba (carnation family) is a characteristic, usually perennial, weed
found on the edges of cornfields on chalk downs or other good well-drained
soils, which flowers from May to September. Its pure white petals are
scented in the evening, which attracts the moths that pollinate it. Male and
female flowers are on different plants; the males have a cylindrical calyx
tube with 10 ribs and 10 stamens; the females have a swollen calyx tube,
which can accommodate the seed-filled capsule, with 20 ribs. The flowering stems may be up to 1 metre tall. Sometimes pale pink flowered plants
can be found which are hybrids with Red Campion. These are common
along hedges, and are normally pollinated by butterflies or bees.

White Campion is found throughout the British Isles, but is rarer in the
north and in the west of Ireland. It never occurs in great quantity, but is
very persistent, being resistant to the selective weedkillers 2–4D and
MCPA.

Dove's-foot Cranesbill photographed 28 May

Dove's-foot Cranesbill seedlings photographed 10 March

Dove's-foot Cranesbill

Geranium molle (geranium family) is a common weed of sandy soils and is found at the edges of arable fields, in gardens, especially on gravel paths, and in open places such as dunes and roadsides by the sea. It is an annual, usually germinating in autumn and over-wintering as a rosette before flowering from April onwards, the flowering branches radiating from the centre. It is common throughout the British Isles and Europe, and across Asia to the Himalayas. It is naturalised in North and South America and in New Zealand.

One of two other species are sometimes found as weeds. The commonest of them is *G. dissectum*, **Cut-leaved Cranesbill**, which differs from Dove's-foot in its more upright stems, more deeply divided leaves and lobed not bifid petals.

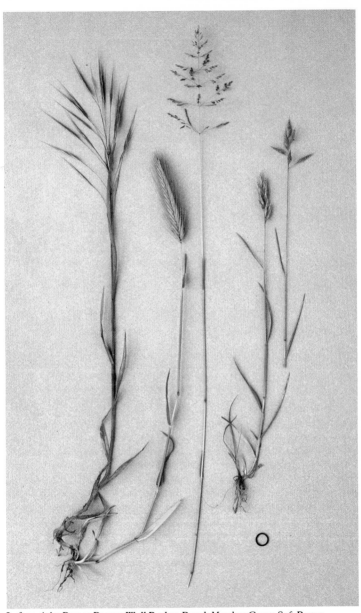

Left to right *Barren Brome; Wall Barley; Rough Meadow Grass; Soft Brome*
photographed 20 May

Couch Grass photographed 6 July

**Barren Brome, Soft Brome, Rough Meadow Grass,
Wall Barley and Couch Grass**

These are some of the commonest grasses which appear as weeds in gardens or in bare soil by roadsides and other waste places.

Barren Brome (*Bromus sterilis*) is soft when young, with long untidy leaves often infected with a white rust. The spikelets hang down gracefully. **Soft Brome** or **Lop Grass** (*Bromus mollis*) has soft fat spikelets with shorter awns which are nodding rather than pendulous. The leaves are softly hairy. **Rough Meadow Grass** (*Poa trivialis*) has leaf sheafs which are rough if rubbed upwards. It is commoner in damper richer ground. **Wall Barley** (*Hordeum murinum*) prefers very dry places. The leaves are slightly hairy on both surfaces and the upper leaf sheath is swollen. **Couch Grass** or **Twitch** (*Elymus repens*) is one of the most persistent of perennial garden weeds. It spreads underground by white, sharp-pointed rhizomes, putting up, at intervals, tufts of the characteristic bluish-green leaves.

Field Penny-cress photographed 16 May

Field Penny-cress seedling photographed 10 March

Field Penny-cress

Thlaspi arvense (cabbage family) is an annual weed of dry fields and bare roadsides. It is easily recognised by its stiff, upright stems which are branched at the base and well furnished with almost circular fruits, 12–22mm in diameter, that are notched at the apex. It is common throughout the British Isles, except in the far north, and through Europe to Siberia and Japan and south to North Africa. The seeds usually germinate in early spring, but also in autumn, and flowering begins in May, lasting until July, the stem reaching at most 30cm in height.

Field Penny-cress is not considered native in the British Isles, but seeds of it have been found in Roman deposits at Silchester and commonly in the Iron Age in Denmark.

Corn Spurry photographed 4 July

Corn Spurry; young plant photographed 20 April

Corn Spurry

Spergula arvensis (carnation family) is a worldwide weed that is very common on poor sandy soils. It is particularly tolerant of very acid soils and will thrive where the pH is as low as 4, too acid for most other crops. An annual, it has narrow leaves in dense tufts that are easy to recognise. The seeds mostly germinate in autumn and flowering takes place from June onwards.

A large-seeded variety, var. *sativa*, has been cultivated for its seeds, and in Shetland where it is called Ureal Plant, these were eaten. It is also used to feed poultry and has been cultivated as cattle fodder. Corn Spurry is known only as a weed of cultivation and has been found in Roman and more recent deposits. It now grows throughout the British Isles, and is especially common in Scotland.

Common Sow Thistle photographed 18 June

Common Sow Thistle; overwintered rosette photographed 5 April

Sow Thistle

Sonchus oleraceus is a very common garden weed; it is usually annual and seeds may germinate in autumn to form a rosette of greyish leaves, or in spring. It has a deep and very tough tap root and soft fleshy leaves, so is difficult to pull up. The leaves, however, make a good salad. **Common Sow Thistle** (shown here) has deeply divided leaves, usually glaucous and without spines. **Prickly Sow Thistle** (*S. asper*) is almost as common and has less deeply divided leaves, edged with soft prickles. Both have small dandelion-like flowers of rather pale yellow from May onwards, but a third weedy species, **Corn Sow Thistle** (*S. arvensis*) has larger flowers, of a rich golden yellow and is a perennial with creeping underground stems which run about near the surface.

All three species are found throughout the British Isles, Europe and North Africa eastwards, and elsewhere as weeds of cultivated land.

71

Hedge Mustard photographed 23 June

Hedge Mustard; young plant photographed 10 April

Hedge Mustard

Sisymbrium officinale (cabbage family) is a common wayside weed through-out the British Isles. It can be recognised by its candelabra-like habit of growth; the very small yellow flowers are in a tight head at the top of the stems, the narrow straight seed pods point upwards and are pressed against the stem. Germination of the seed can be in autumn or spring, and the plant usually flowers in June and July.

Hedge Mustard is not of great significance as a weed, but it can be a host of the cabbage disease, Club Root, and enable that disease to survive even where cabbages or other *Brassica* species are not being cultivated.

It is found throughout Europe and South Africa, to Western Asia, and is naturalised in North and South America, South Africa, Australia and New Zealand.

Shepherd's Needle photographed 20 May

Shepherd's Needle photographed 20 May

Shepherd's Needle

Scandix pecten-veneris (celery family) is one of the harmless and attractive weeds that has almost become extinct in recent years with improvements in agriculture and increased use of weedkillers. It was formerly common, especially in southern and eastern England, but we had to go to France to find the specimen shown here.

The seeds germinate in autumn; flowering begins in April and continues through the summer. The fruits are the most conspicuous part of the plant, and may be 70mm long in an upright cluster: it is they that give the plant its ancient names of Shepherd's or Puck's Needle, or Venus's Comb.

On the Continent, Shepherd's Needle is found from Sweden south-wards and across Asia to the Himalayas. It is a weed of cultivated land also in the southern hemisphere.

Sheep's Sorrel photographed 10 July

Sheep's Sorrel; overwintered rosette photographed 16 April

Sheep's Sorrel

Rumex acetosella (polygonum family) is a small creeping version of the Common Sorrel. It is usually found as a weed on light sandy soils and creeps underground with very slender roots forming loose patches. The reddish flowering stems are usually less than 30cm high, and other differences from Common Sorrel are the stalked upper leaves and spear-shaped lower leaves with forward pointing lobes. Three microspecies are recognised in the British Isles. These differ in the width of their leaves, the size of their fruit and in chromosome number.

Sheep's Sorrel flowers from May onwards, the males and females on separate plants; the leaves taste acidic as well as bitter. It is common throughout the British Isles, usually on acid soils though it will grow happily in bare places on chalky sands. It is found throughout Europe and across Asia and North Africa, as well as in temperate parts of the southern hemisphere.

Oxalis (O. corymbosa) *photographed 11 July*

Oxalis leaves growing from bulbils photographed 18 June

Oxalis

Several species of Oxalis (oxalis family) from the southern hemisphere have recently become pests in British gardens.

O. corniculata, is small, creeping, with bright yellow flowers; var. *microphylla* is an even smaller form originating in Tasmania and New Zealand. *O. europaea*, upright, annual, or sometimes with stolons, has yellow flowers. *O. corymbosa* (shown here) has a swollen rootstock with several (c. 20) bulbils on top which may be at some depth, leaflets 2.5–5cm wide, sparsely hairy, heartshaped, with a deep narrow indentation, purplish-pink flowers. *O. latifolia* has a swollen rootstock with a few bulbils on long stolons, leaflets 2–4.5cm across, with a wide shallow indentation, and diverging lobes, pink flowers. *O. pes-caprae*, the **Bermuda Buttercup**, is a beautiful species, but frost tender. A native of South Africa, it is a weed around the Mediterranean and along the west coast of Britain.

Goosegrass photographed 12 June

Goosegrass; young plants photographed 18 May

Goosegrass or Cleavers

Galium aparine (madder family) is very common in shady gardens, hedges, fields, and other open habitats throughout the British Isles, Europe and western Asia and is widely introduced elsewhere. The stems may spread up to 120cm, clambering over other plants and smothering them. The edges of the leaves and corner of the stems are covered with small downward pointing spikes so they feel sticky, and the round seeds have hooked hairs with swollen bases which stick to clothing or passing animals.

Goosegrass is an annual, the seeds germinating in autumn or spring and the plant growing very quickly in early summer. The whorls of narrow leaves are typical of the bedstraws, as are the tiny 4-petalled flowers.

G. tricornutum with flower stalks strongly recurred, and the fruits not adhesive, is sometimes found as a weed in cornfields and other dry places.

Small Toadflax photographed 12 September

Small Toadflax; young plants photographed 10 May

Small Toadflax

Chaenorrhinum minus (figwort family) is one of a group of small summer annuals which can be found in the stubble of harvested cornfields. It is commonest on chalk and so is frequently found in southern England and on the limestone soils of central Ireland. As well as cornfields, it can be found by roadsides and in other bare ground and especially along gravelly railway tracks. The whole plant is covered with sticky glandular hairs, and the flowers are like tiny greyish-purple snapdragons. The seeds germinate in late spring and flowering lasts from July to October.

Most *Chaenorrhinum* species are rock plants of the Mediterranean region, and Small Toadflax itself is commoner in southern Europe and across southern Asia to India, than in the north.

Fluellen photographed 12 September

Fluellen photographed 28 September

Fluellen

Kickxia elatine (figwort family) is a creeping annual common in cornfields, normally on the chalk, and in other waste places. Like Small Toadflax, to which it is closely related, Fluellen may be found flowering among stubble, though early ploughing and stubble burning have made it much rarer than even a few years ago. It is easily recognised by its arrow-head shaped leaves and its bright yellow and purple snapdragon flowers with straight spurs on long hairy stalks.

A second species, sometimes distinguished as **Male Fluellen** (*K. spuria*), differs in having leaves rounded at the base, and flowers with curved spurs on smooth stalks. The seeds of both species germinate in spring and flowering starts in July and continues in warm autumns until the frost. Both species are commonest in southern England and only *K. elatine* is found in Ireland. In Europe they are also commoner in the south and around the Mediterranean.

Daisy photographed 6 May

Daisy; rosette in lawn photographed 10 March

Daisy

Bellis perennis (daisy family), is common throughout the British Isles, across Europe and in western Asia. It is most familiar as a weed of lawns, though it can also seed itself all over flower beds, especially if lawn mowings are used as a mulch. It flowers from about March to October and as a wild flower it is common on downs or along roadsides especially on alkaline soils or in short grass in meadows where it can be a lovely sight on a fine morning in May. Most people now consider a certain number of daisies to be an ornament to any lawn, but if the infestation is too dense, they can easily be reduced by sulphate of ammonia which scorches the daisy leaves and encourages the grass or by using 2–4D in a lawn weedkiller.

The Daisy is so called because the flowers open only on warm or sunny days and close in the evening, hence Day's Eye. The flowers can be used to make wine.

Scarlet Pimpernel photographed 22 May

Scarlet Pimpernel photographed 12 July

Scarlet Pimpernel

Anagallis arvensis (primrose family) is conspicuous when its bright red flowers are open in the sun, but vanishes into the background when they are closed. They normally open about eight in the morning in warm sunny weather, and close in the afternoon or if it becomes cold or wet.

Scarlet Pimpernel is common as a cornfield weed, especially on light soils in the south of England, Europe and in all temperate parts of the world. Its seeds germinate in autumn or early spring, and flowering starts in June. The flowers have stamens with hairy stalks, and are usually red, but may be blue, lilac, flesh-coloured or even white: the blue variety is the least rare, but even that is very seldom seen in England, though it is commoner on the Continent.

89

Corn Cockle photographed 16 July

Corn Cockle photographed 16 July

Corn Cockle

Agrostemma githago (carnation family), one of the most beautiful of cornfield weeds, was common throughout the British Isles until this century, but is now almost extinct here as a weed, and probably only survives where it is treasured in gardens. It is known in deposits of Roman Age in southern England and in the 16th century it was a menace as its large seeds, which are poisonous, were a common contaminant of rye or wheat and often made the flour inedible, and those who ate it susceptible to leprosy. Improved methods of cleaning grain lead to its disappearance from seed corn, and contributed to its rapid decline from the end of the 19th century.

The seeds germinate in May and flowering is from June to August. Corn Cockle is known as a weed in all temperate areas of the world, but probably originated with agriculture in Turkey, where a second species, *A. gracile*, is found.

Top left to bottom right *Sycamore; Plane; Sallow; Cherry, photographed 20 July*

Left *Buddleia*; right *Laburnum, photographed 20 July*

Tree Seedlings

Many common garden trees seed themselves and their seedlings are often difficult to recognise when the adult leaf shapes have not developed. Those shown here were found in a London square in summer. Most came from trees fruiting in the area, but some may have come in with soil.

London Plane, *Platanus* × *hispanica*; although it is probably a hybrid between the Asiatic and America species, it is fertile and produces abundant seedlings in mid-summer. **Sycamore**, *Acer pseudoplatanus*; the winged fruits parachute down in autumn and germinate immediately or in early spring, the elongated cotyledous appearing in April. **Sallow**, *Salix capraea*; the seeds of this species are very light and supported by long silky hairs so can blow long distances from the parent. It is common as a weed, and is often seen on the bare ground of new road works. **Wild Cherry**, *Prunus avium*; birds help to spread cherry stones some distance from the parent trees. The leaves can be recognised by the two glands at their base. **Buddleia**, *B. davidii*; recognised by its opposite leaves, it was introduced from China in 1896. The seeds, which are very light, can be blown long distances, and come up in unexpected places such as on walls or in gutters. **Laburnum**, *L. anagyroides*; the black seeds of Laburnum are deadly poisonous and germinate freely, producing first two rather fat cotyledons.

93

Annual Mercury photographed 18 July

Annual Mercury photographed 21 July

Annual Mercury

Mercurialis annua (spurge family) is a characteristic late summer annual in London gardens, being commonest on light sandy soils. It is also common elsewhere in the south, but is not found at all north of Lancashire. Germination of the seeds is from May onwards, and flowering, which has been found to depend on a sufficient number of warm nights, usually starts in July. Male and female flowers are on different plants, though occasionally a hermaphrodite plant may appear.

  Dog's Mercury (*Mercurialis perennis*), normally a woodland plant, is also a serious weed in gardens. It spreads underground by white brittle rhizomes and is difficult to remove entirely. It can be spread at least a foot in one season. Unlike Annual Mercury, it flowers in early spring, so the two are unlikely to be confused.

Stinging Nettle: left *female*; right *male, photographed 4 July*

Stinging Nettle photographed 19 March   *Annual Nettle photographed 15 June*

Stinging Nettles

Urtica dioica (nettle family) is the commonest perennial Stinging Nettle found in waste places, especially around old buildings, by roadsides, or in the mountains in places where sheep congregate. Its seeds and pollen have been found in ancient deposits dating from before the last ice age. Male and female flowers are on separate plants, and cross pollination is by wind. The young shoots are very nutritious and can be eaten like spinach, or made into soup or beer.

Small Nettle, *U. urens* (stinking) is an annual garden or field weed, common throughout the British Isles, especially in soils high in nitrogen and slightly acidic. The seeds mostly germinate in spring and flowering is from June to September though plants can over-winter and be found in flower in early spring. It also has a sting. Both nettles are common around the northern hemisphere, and the Stinging Nettle is found in all temperate regions of the world.

Broad-leaved Dock photographed 21 July

Broad-leaved Dock seedling photographed 20 April

Docks

Rumex obtusifolius (polygonum family), the **Broad-leaved Dock**, is one of several weedy species. They are all perennials with deep tap roots which are difficult to pull up, and sprout again if broken. The seeds are very long lived; 52 per cent germination was had in seeds of *R. crispus* that had been underground for 50 years. Broad-leaved Dock may be recognised by its 3 long-toothed triangular perianth segments, one of which has a prominent lump in the middle. **Curled Dock** (*R. crispus*) has smooth or wavy-edged triangular perianth segments, each with a lump; a third species *R. conglomeratus* has the flowers in clusters, well separated from one another, and smaller narrower perianth segments, each with a lump.

Dock seeds usually germinate in spring, and flowering is from June onwards, or a month later in *R. conglomeratus*. All three species are common throughout the British Isles.

Corn Marigold photographed 8 July

Corn Marigold photographed 16 July

Corn Marigold or Guildweed

Chrysanthemum segetum (daisy family) was probably originally native to the Mediterranean region, but has been a weed of cornfields in England since at least Roman times. It is now found throughout Europe from Norway southwards, and as a weed in North and South America. Formerly common throughout the British Isles, it is now distinctly less rare on sandy soils in East Anglia, the Midlands, in the West of Scotland and in Ireland. It is often considered an indicator of calcium deficiency, but also requires well-drained conditions. Germination may take place in autumn but is commoner in spring and flowering is induced by long days, from June to September. Its waxy bluish-green leaves help protect it from herbicides, but is still a fast diminishing species, probably because of better cleaning of seed.

Self-heal photographed 16 July

Self-heal, growing in a lawn, photographed 16 July

Self-heal

Prunella vulgaris (dead-nettle family) forms mats of dark green leaves on lawns, and its dark purple flowers are produced so close to the ground that they escape the mower. As a wild plant, Self-heal is common in damp pastures and clearings, and along rides in woods throughout the British Isles, usually on base-rich soils, flowering from June to September.

The flowers, which can sometimes be pink or white, are either large and bisexual or smaller and female. The name Self-heal refers to the plant's reputation as a wound-herb, which it shares with the rather similar Bugle.

A second species of *Prunella*, *P. laciniata* is native to central and southern Europe, and is naturalised in southern England, being recorded there first in 1887. It has creamy-white flowers and dissected upper leaves, occasionally with only one lobe.

Pale Persicaria photographed 30 July

Persicaria seedling photographed 20 May

Persicaria or Red Shank

Two species of Persicaria (polygonum family), *Polygonum persicaria*, **Pink Persicaria**, and *P. lapathifolium*, **Pale Persicaria** (shown here), are common weeds, especially in rather damp soil, in gardens, in arable crops such as potatoes and in drying mud by ponds and are found throughout the British Isles and across the northern hemisphere.

Germination takes place in late spring or early summer, and they flower from June onwards. Pink Persicaria is usually glabrous with pink flowers, while Pale Persicaria is hairy with greenish-white glandular flowers.

The seeds of Persicaria are edible, being closely related to Buckwheat (*Fagopyrum esculentum*) and large numbers of Pale Persicaria seeds were found in the stomach of Tollund Man who lived in the early Iron Age, along with *Camelina sativa* a yellow mustard still sometimes cultivated as an oil seed.

Knot Grass photographed 8 July

Knot Grass photographed 10 June

Knotgrass

Polygonum aviculare (polygonum family) is common in waste places, especially in sandy soils, and as a weed. It consists of four microspecies.

P. boreale is known only from Shetland to the Arctic. *P. rurivagum* has narrow, linear-lanceolate stem-leaves, 1–4mm broad, and fruits which are exserted from the perianth. It is confined to chalky cornfields in the south of England and western Europe. *P. arenastrum* is a creeping plant with the branch and stem-leaves equal, the perianth segments united for half their length and small fruits up to 2.5mm long. It is common everywhere on dry soils. *P. aviculare* itself is an erect or spreading plant with perianth segments united only at the base, and fruit 2.5–3.5mm long. It is common throughout Britain, Europe, Asia and as a weed in North and South America and Australasia.

Black Bindweed photographed 14 August

Black Bindweed seedling photographed 20 May

Black Bindweed

Fallopia convolvulus (polygonum family) is also known under the generic names *Bilderdykia* and *Polygonum*. It is a common annual weed in corn-fields, less often in gardens and waste places, with a twining stem, convolvulus-like leaves, *Polygonum*-like flowers and triangular fruit.

Seeds germinate in early summer, and flowering is from July to October. It is found commonly throughout the British Isles, but always in man-made habitats, and all the fossil records are associated with cultivation from the late Bronze Age onwards. On the Continent, Black Bindweed is everywhere common south to North Africa and east-wards across Asia; it is recorded as a weed in North America and South Africa.

Greater Plantain photographed 18 July

Greater Plantain seedling photographed 10 July

Greater Plantain or Waybread

Plantago major (plantain family) is a perennial which, as its alternative name suggests, is very common along paths, tracks and by roadsides. Its flat tough leaves can tolerate trampling and its flower stems will spring up again after being flattened. Its seeds are very long lived and have been shown to germinate after 40 years. They become sticky when wet, and this, as well as their palatability to sparrows and other seed-eating birds, aids their dispersal.

A second plantain species, with broad leaves, is sometimes found in lawns, especially on the chalk or limestone soils. This is **Hoary Plantain**, *P. media*, which has short and rather attractive pinkish flower heads and hairy leaves.

Greater Plantain is common throughout the British Isles, and Europe and is known as a weed throughout the world.

left *Field Poppy;* right *Long-headed Poppy, photographed 8 July*

Field Poppies photographed 8 July

Field Poppy

Papaver rhoeas (poppy family) is the commonest of the red poppies found in cornfields and by roadsides, and grows throughout the British Isles, Europe and North Africa, except in the far north. In all, five species occur in Britain. They may be recognised by their seed capsules; short and smooth in *P. rhoeas*, long and smooth in the **long-headed poppies** *P. dubium* and *P. lecoqii*, short and bristly in *P. hybridum* and long and bristly in *P. argemone* (p. 2). The long smooth-headed poppies also have paler, more orange-red flowers and can be told apart by the colour of their milky juice, white in *P. dubium*, yellow in *P. lecoqii*. The bristly-headed poppies are rather rare, the others are still common.

Field Poppy seeds normally germinate in spring, those of long-headed poppies in autumn, but they are capable of prolonged dormancy in the soil.

Dwarf Mallow seedling photographed 14 August

Dwarf Mallow photographed 14 August

Dwarf Mallow

Malva neglecta (mallow family) is a frequent plant of roadsides and waste places though less common as a cornfield or garden weed. It grows throughout the British Isles, but is rarer in the north and far west. It is found in Europe, North Africa and Asia, and as a weed in North America.

Usually an annual, it commonly germinates in spring. It is a creeping plant with rather small, whitish flowers with darker veins which appear from June to September. **Common Mallow** (*M. sylvestris*) has larger rose-purple flowers with darker stripes, 2.5–4cm in diameter, and is usually a perennial. It is also common in waste places and by roads. Two other small-flowered, European species are sometimes found in Britain. *M. pusilla* has flowers only 5cm in diameter with a green fruiting calyx. *M. parviflora* has equally small flowers with a calyx which enlarges and becomes scarious in fruit.

Nipplewort photographed 18 July

Nipplewort; overwintered rosette photographed 10 April

Nipplewort

Lapsana communis (daisy family) is commonly found as a weed throughout the British Isles, Europe, North Africa and west and central Asia, in gardens, on waste ground and in hedges, usually on heavier soils. It is a relative of the lettuce and was, in the past, eaten as a salad vegetable, though it is rather bitter. The seeds germinate in autumn and spring, and flowering starts in July, a strong rosette of leaves being built up before the flowering stem elongates.

A second species of *Lapsana*, *L. intermedia*, a native of the Caucasus and eastern Europe, has narrow linear upper leaves and larger flower heads, and has been recorded in Bedfordshire.

The name Nipplewort is, according to Geoffrey Grigson, derived from Camerarius, *Hortus medicus et Philosophicus* 1588, where the plant was called Papillaris, because it was good to heal ulcers of the nipples.

Gallant Soldier photographed 18 August

Gallant Soldier seedlings photographed 20 April

Gallant Soldier

Galinsoga parviflora (daisy family) has been common in London gardens for some time, having been first recorded as a weed in Richmond in 1860. It had escaped from Kew Gardens where it was grown as a botanical curiosity having come from Peru. It is now found scattered throughout southern England, but is still commonest in London. The very closely related *G. ciliata* shown here has appeared more recently, but now seems to be commoner. It is said to differ in the hairier upper part of the stem.

The fruits from the disc florets are topped by rough hairy bristles and may become attached to clothing; the marginal florets produce a rather inefficient parachute. Germination is in spring, but more than one generation may be produced during the summer.

Gallant Soldier is a corruption of the Latin name *Galinsoga*.

Top to bottom Epilobium adenocaulon; E. lanceolatum; E. roseum; E. hirsutum, *photographed 18 August*

Willowherb; overwintered rosettes photographed 4 May

Willowherbs

Epilobium species (willowherb family) belong to the same family as *Fuchsia*. The family resemblance can be seen in the young shoots of the two plants, if not in the flowers. Several species are common as weeds in shady damp places in gardens; their flowers have a white stigma which may be divided or club-shaped; their seeds are suspended on silky threads.

Great Hairy Willowherb or **Codlins-and-Cream** (*E. hirsutum*) is a common wild flower by streams and in ditches and has stems up to 150cm high. **Small-flowered Willowherb** (*E. roseum*) has a club-shaped stigma and leaves with a stalk 3–20mm long. *E. adenocaulon* has a club-shaped stigma, and leaves with a very short stalk 1.5–3mm long. It is a native of North America, first recorded in 1891, but now widely naturalised. *E. lanceolatum* has a divided stigma, and leaves with stalks 4–8mm long.

below left *Lesser Swine-cress*; above right *Swine-cress, photographed 16 July*

Swine-cress; young plant photographed 23 May

Swine-cress

Coronopus didymus (cabbage family) is a common annual in gardens and waste places, especially in southern England and Ireland. It was probably originally native to South America, but has been known in Britain since the end of the 18th century, and is now found all over the world. The seeds germinate in early summer and flowering begins in July.

Closely related but distinct in appearance is the **Swine-cress**, *Coronopus squamatus*, a flat creeping weed common on paths and other places where trampling reduces competition from taller plants. It has been found in Roman deposits in southern England, so is probably a native, and is today found everywhere, though remains rare in the north and west. It has more coarsely divided leaves, and larger but fewer flowers and fruits. It is found throughout Europe and as a weed in other temperate regions of the world.

Fat Hen photographed 14 August

Fat Hen seedling photographed 10 June

Fat Hen

Chenopodium album (goosefoot family) is the commonest of the goosefoots in most gardens. It is found also in waste places, and in cornfields, especially around manure heaps, throughout Britain, Europe, Asia and temperate areas of the southern hemisphere.

When young the plant has a whitish dusty appearance, due to the small, almost spherical, hairs. The name Fat Hen refers to the use of the plant for fattening chickens, but it was also grown as a vegetable in eastern Europe and Russia. The leaves can be eaten like spinach, the seeds, which have been found in Roman and Bronze Age deposits, used as grain.

Orache *Atriplex patula*, and *A. hastata* have a similar mealy covering. Both are also common, but may be distinguished from *Chenopodium* by the large triangular bracteoles which enclose their fruit.

left *Red Goosefoot;* right *Many-seeded Goosefoot, photographed 12 September*

Many-seeded Goosefoot seedling photographed 18 July

Red Goosefoot, Many-seeded Goosefoot

Chenopodium rubrum and *C. polyspermum* (goosefoot family) are two annual species with green, not mealy leaves, often suffused with red. Many-seeded Goosefoot is recognised by its rounded, untoothed leaves of a rather thin texture (occasionally they have about one shallow tooth on each side), and black seeds. Red Goosefoot has much toothed leaves of a thick fleshy texture, and red brown seeds. Both species are found as garden weeds, or in fields, especially those which have been manured, and they vary greatly in size according to the richness of the soil. The seeds germinate in late spring and summer and flowering is from July till October. Both species are commonest in southern England and rarer in the north and west. Only Red Goosefoot is common in Ireland.

Both species are found throughout Europe, into Asia and as weeds in North America.

Cornflower photographed 16 July

Cornflower photographed 16 July

Cornflower

Centaurea cyanus (daisy family) is one of the beautiful cornfield weeds which is now almost extinct as a weed, but treasured in gardens. Formerly it was common throughout the British Isles, especially on lighter, more acidic soils. Since about 1925, however, it has become very rare, probably for a combination of factors including a decline in the acreage of rye, with which both Cornflower and Corncockle were associated, the improvements in seed cleaning, the greater rarity of imported seed, and the increased use of selective weedkillers in cornfields.

Cornflower seeds germinate either in autumn and over-winter, or in spring, and flowering starts in June.

On the Continent Cornflowers are still frequent, especially around the Mediterranean and in Western Asia.

Fool's Parsley photographed 16 July

Fool's Parsley seedling photographed 23 May

Fool's Parsley

Aethusa cynapium (celery family) is a common garden weed which is found also in cornfields and waste places. The plant is easily recognised by the dark green downward pointing bracts below the umbel, and the white flowers. The leaves are dark green, finely divided like those of ordinary, not crisped parsley, and have an acrid smell.

Fool's Parsley is an annual; some seeds may germinate in autumn and over-winter, but most germinate in spring: flowering is mostly in July and August. The leaves are very poisonous as they contain conine, the active constituent of Hemlock, hence the name Fool's Parsley.

Fool's Parsley is common throughout the British Isles, except in the extreme north, across Europe to the Caucasus and in North Africa. It is known as a weed from North America.

Ground Elder photographed 18 June

Ground Elder; young leaves photographed 6 May

Ground Elder, Bishop's Weed, Goutweed or Herb Gerard

Aegopodium podagraria (celery family) is a most pernicious garden weed once it becomes established. Its alternative names, Ground Elder in England and Bishop's Weed in Scotland, do not refer to its evil properties as a weed, but to its appearance and to its frequent association with old monastic sites. It was a popular pot herb in medieval times and a remedy for gout. From this are derived its other names, for it was dedicated to St Gerard, the patron saint of gout sufferers. Ground Elder has been known in Britain since Roman times and was probably introduced here by the Romans as a vegetable. It is native to mountain woods, in Europe, Turkey and in the Caucasus, where I have seen it in dense birch forest far from any habitation, but it is now found throughout the British Isles and most of Europe, except the south and eastwards into Siberia.

Weasel's Snout photographed 18 July

Weasel's Snout photographed 15 July

Weasel's Snout, Calf's Snout or Corn Snapdragon

Misopates orontium (figwort family) is now a rare weed of cornfields, roadsides and waste places on sandy soils. Formerly it was common in suitable places in southern England, and south-west Wales and in parts of Co. Cork, but now survives mainly in collections of ancient weeds. It is found on the Continent especially in southern Europe, around the Mediterranean to Ethiopia and across Asia to the Himalayas. The seeds germinate late, not till May or June, and flowering is from July to October. It has been found to set seed well only after a hot summer, so a series of wet summers could greatly reduce its numbers.

The only closely related species in Britain is the Snapdragon, *Antirrhinum majus*, a perennial native on rocks in the Mediterranean region. It is like a smaller version of a garden antirrhinum, and usually has reddish-purple flowers and is found on old city walls.

Corn Mint photographed 14 August

Corn Mint; young leaves photographed 10 May

Corn Mint

Mentha arvensis (dead-nettle family) is a common perennial weed throughout the British Isles and across most of Europe and Asia to the Himalayas.
It grows on the edges of cornfields, especially on heavy lime-rich soils, in
waste places and on the dried up mud of ponds and reservoirs, flowering
from May to October. It can be distinguished from other mints by its
flowers which are in separate whorls in the axils of leaf-like bracts. Even
the uppermost bracts are longer than the flowers. Its smell is not strong,
but rather sweet.

Where Corn Mint grows near water, the hybrid between it and Water
Mint (*M. aquatica*) is common. It is called *M. X verticillata* and has the
upper flowers crowded with short bracts, and longer tubular calices with
long teeth.

Marsh Cudweed photographed 18 July

Marsh Cudweed seedling photographed 23 May

Marsh Cudweed

Filaginella uliginosa (daisy family) is a small, low, woolly annual found throughout the British Isles and across the Continent to western Asia and is also known as a weed in North America. It is common on poorly drained soils such as in muddy ruts and entrances of fields, in places where cattle have trampled the ground in winter, on the dried mud of ponds and reservoirs or in gardens on heavy soil. The seeds germinate in early summer and flowering is from July onwards.

Other species of cudweed are commoner in dry acid sandy soils. They are more upright, slender plants with erect leaves and heads in clusters. *F. germanica* has 20–40 heads in rounded sessile clusters, while *F. minima*, Slender Cudweed, has 3–6 heads in longer clusters. Other species are much rarer.

Petty Spurge photographed 20 April

Caper Spurge seedlings photographed 23 April

Petty Spurge

Euphorbia peplus (spurge family), is the commonest of weedy spurges, found everywhere throughout the British Isles, Europe and western Asia, in all kinds of arable and waste ground. It is often infected with a pale orange rust. Like all spurges it has a poisonous milky juice.

Also shown here are seedlings of **Caper Spurge** (*E. lathyrus*). They appear in gardens in summer, and quickly form striking stiff upright plants with four rows of leaves. The following year they become huge, candalabra-like plants with green flowers, pointed bracts and swollen puffy caper-like fruits which are poisonous. Caper Spurge is possibly native in woods in southern England and Wales, but is commoner as a weed in old gardens where its appearance is interestingly sporadic. It is found also in southern Europe as far north as Germany.

Sun Spurge photographed 14 August

Dwarf Spurge photographed 24 August

Sun Spurge, Dwarf Spurge

Euphorbia helioscopia, Sun Spurge, can make a large plant about 30cm high and across, with very rounded leaves which may be bright yellowish, especially in the inflorescence. Its glands are oval, not curved and horned like those of the Petty Spurge (p. 141). It is common throughout the British Isles and Europe, especially in heavy limey soils, and among root crops such as potatoes. Its seeds germinate in spring and summer, but it can over-winter and be found in flower at any time of year.

Dwarf Spurge (*E. exigua*) is a rarer plant, most frequently seen in the stubble of cornfields, especially on chalk and limestone in south-eastern England and in Ireland. Its bluish-green narrow leaves are unmistakeable and its glands are curved, with long horns. It is found throughout Europe except in the far north, and around the Mediterranean.

Large-flowered Hemp-nettle photographed 12 July

Hemp-nettle seedling photographed 6 June

Hemp-nettles

Galeopsis speciosa (dead-nettle family) is a striking annual weed of cornfields and waste places, commonest on acid soils and in northern England, Scotland and Ireland. It can be distinguished from most other hemp-nettles by its large pale yellow and purple flowers; the very rare *G. segetum* has equally large flowers, but lacks the purple lip and has velvety silky leaves. Most of the other species of *Galeopsis* usually have small pinkish-purple flowers; *G. tetrahit* is common throughout the British Isles; *G. angustifolia* with narrow leaves, is commonest on the chalk in southern and eastern England.

Creeping Buttercup photographed 6 June

Creeping Buttercup photographed 2 July

Creeping Buttercup

Ranunculus repens (buttercup family) is a common garden weed, especially in good damp soil, but it is also sometimes found as a cornfield weed. The plant spreads by runners and can emerge from the lawn and rush across the flower bed rooting and making young plants as it goes. In one season a plant has been measured to cover about 3 square metres. It also seeds freely.

Two other common meadow buttercups are sometimes found as garden or lawn weeds. *R. acris* has deeply divided basal leaves, the middle lobe not much longer than the side lobes, and sepals pressed up under the petals. *R. bulbosus* has a tuberous base to the stem and leaves, the middle leaf-like lobe a little longer than the side lobes and reflexed sepals.

All 3 species are found commonly throughout Britain, across central Europe and into Asia, but are rarer in the south.

Yellow Forget-me-not photographed 10 August

Yellow Forget-me-not photographed 10 August

Yellow Forget-me-not

Amsinkia intermedia (borage family) is the most likely of the yellow-flowered bugloss-like plants to be found growing in the British Isles. It is native of America and was probably brought here with Californian seed. It was first found in chicken-runs in East Anglia before 1920 and has since been recorded in many counties in southern England, although it is still commonest in Suffolk where our specimen was collected. It is found as a cornfield weed, especially in sandy ground. The seedlings can be recognised by their 2-lobed hairy cotyledons. The seeds are often held in the fallen calyx and that can cling to clothing or on to passing animals; *Amsinkia* is one of the species which has been introduced with wool shoddy, which is sometimes used as fertiliser, and as a contaminant of bird-seed mixtures.

Basil Thyme photographed 20 August

Basil Thyme with Charlock and Scarlet Pimpernel photographed 15 July

Basil Thyme

Acinos arvensis (dead-nettle family) is a frequent weed of the chalk, especially in southern England, and less common on limestone in Ireland and as far north as Inverness. It is found in cornfields, on roadsides and rocks, and in thin grasslands such as the sides of chalk pits. It is an annual and flowers from May onwards. Its purplish flowers with white markings on the lower lip make it easy to recognise. On the Continent it is found across Europe to Greece and the Caucasus.

The rather similar Wild Basil, *Clinopodium vulgare*, is also found commonly on the chalk. It is a perennial, softly hairy, with much pinker flowers without white markings.

Other species of *Acinos* are found in southern Europe. *A. alpinus* is the commonest and is a sprawling perennial with violet and white flowers.

Larkspur photographed 11 July

Larkspur seedlings photographed 4 May

Larkspur

Consolida orientalis (buttercup family) is a common garden annual which often becomes temporarily naturalised in waste places or in cornfields. It is usually purplish-blue but may be pink or white. It can be distinguished from *C. ambigua*, which was formerly naturalised in cornfields in East Anglia, mainly around Cambridge, by its erect branches, bracteoles inserted above (not below) the middle of the pedicel and its abruptly beaked seed capsule. A third species, *C. regalis*, has glabrous not hairy seed capsules and is much more diffusely branched.

These three species all come into the category of 'casuals'; they may appear in one place for a year or two, but seldom persist longer than that. Like many other casuals, these three *Consolida* species are natives of the Mediterranean and need hotter, drier summers than they normally get in the British Isles.

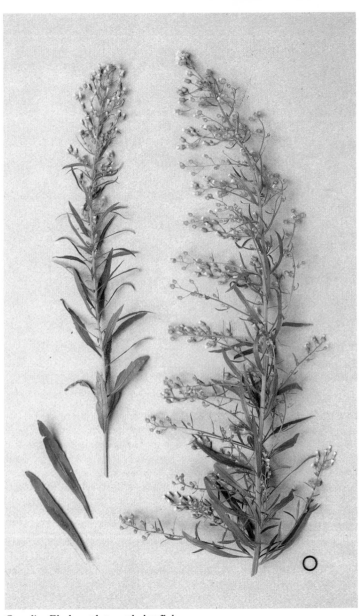

Canadian Fleabane photographed 30 July

Canadian Fleabane seedling photographed 4 May

Canadian Fleabane

Conyza canadensis (daisy family) is a native of North America. It was first recorded as a weed in London in about 1700, and was still rare in 1900, being found mainly around London, in the south of East Anglia, and in Devonshire. It was typically found on railway embankments, and after the War was noticed as a regular colonist, with *Buddleia davidii* (p. 93), of bomb sites. Now it is common over most of south-east England, but not recorded in Ireland or Scotland. The seeds usually germinate in autumn and make a rosette of narrow leaves. Flowering lasts from August to October and each plant may produce on average 50,000 seeds. They are small, with a parachute of bristly hairs and so can be dispersed with ease.

On the Continent Canadian Fleabane is also very common except in the far north.

Black Nightshade photographed 12 September

Black Nightshade photographed 18 August

Black Nightshade

Solanum nigrum (nightshade family) is one of the later common annual weeds to flower and fruit. The seeds germinate in late spring or early summer, and the fruits ripen from August onwards. The flowers are white; it is the purplish-black fruits which give the plant its name. Black Nightshade berries vary greatly in the amount of poisonous alkaloids they contain, and some strains are edible, and made into pies, especially in the Mississippi valley. On the Continent, it is common everywhere, except in the far northern islands.

Other closely related species are found in Europe but rarely in the British Isles. Commonest is *S. luteum* with red, orange or yellow berries and only 3–5 flowers in a cyme. *S. sarrachoides* has a calyx which enlarges in fruit: the berries are green or black. It is found in England, France and Germany.

INDEX

159

Roger Phillips has pioneered the photography of natural history which ensures reliable identification. By placing each specimen against a plain background he is able to show details that would otherwise have been lost if it had been photographed solely *in situ*. Such is the success of his technique that his books, which include the definitive guide to *Mushrooms* and *Wild Food*, have sold over a million copies worldwide. He is also the winner of numerous awards, including three for best produced and best designed books and the André Simon prize for 1983 for *Wild Food*.

Martyn Rix took a degree in botany at Trinity College, Dublin and then went on to Cambridge. After a further period of study in Zurich he became resident botanist at the Royal Horticultural Society's gardens at Wisley for several years. He is now a freelance writer.

Jacqui Hurst studied photography at Gloucestershire College of Art & Design, worked as an assistant to Roger Phillips for 4 years, and is now a freelance journalist and photographer, specialising in country matters.

Acknowledgements
We should like to thank John & Caroline Stevenson of Suffolk Herbs, Little Cornard, for their help in providing specimens of several rare cornfield weeds, which they have preserved.

First published in Great Britain 1986
by Elm Tree Books/Hamish Hamilton Ltd
Garden House 57-59 Long Acre London WC2E 9JZ

Copyright © 1986 by Roger Phillips

Cover design by Pat Doyle

British Library Cataloguing in Publication Data

Phillips, Roger, *1932–*
  Weeds.
  1. Weeds – Identification
  I. Title   II. Rix, Martyn   III. Hurst, Jacqui
  581.6'52   SB611
  ISBN 0-241-11812-3
  ISBN 0-241-11755-0 Pbk

Typeset by Rowland Phototypesetting Ltd, Bury St Edmunds, Suffolk
Printed and bound in Italy by
Arnoldo Mondadori Editore, Verona